Random House All-About Books™

ANIMAL HOMES

Written by Theodore Rowland Entwistle

Designed by David Nash

Illustrated by
Graham Allen, Mike Atkinson,
Roy Coombs, and Susan Neale

Random House 🏠 **New York**

Our earth is the home of many different kinds of animals with many different ways of life. Many grazing animals, such as bison, do not have a settled home. They wander in herds across the plains. Some animals, such as birds, build temporary homes in which to rear their young. Other animals build permanent homes with great skill and care. Prairie dogs dig a network of tunnels in which to hide from their enemies. A "sentry" raises the alarm when an enemy, such as an eagle, attacks.

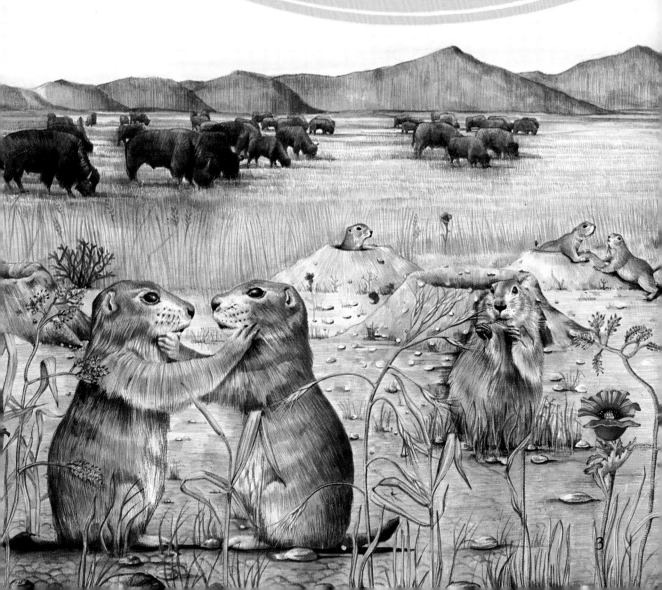

ruby - throated hummingbird

golden oriole

long - tailed tit

woodpecker

tailorbird

wren

The Nest Builders

Birds do not live in nests all the time. They build nests to lay their eggs in and to bring up their young. In this picture there are several kinds of birds' nests. Any tree that held all these nests would be very unusual indeed! But all these nests can be found in trees, though not all in the same part of the world.

One of the cleverest nests is made by the tailorbird from eastern Asia. Using its beak as a needle, it sews the edges of leaves together to make a bag.

Behind the tailorbird is a bowl-shaped nest, the usual type of home built by finches, thrushes, and

sand martin

plover

4

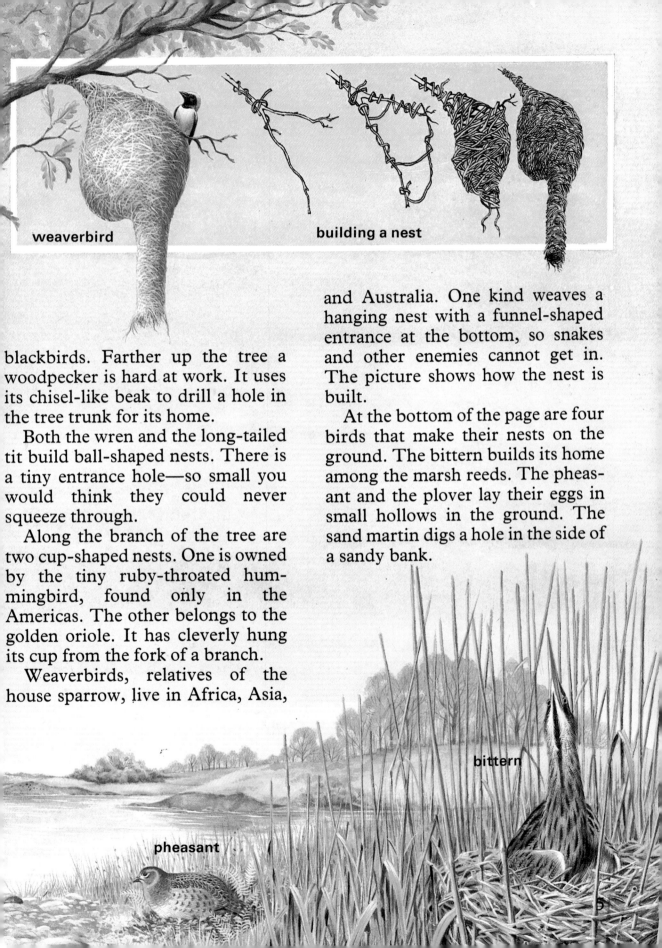

weaverbird

building a nest

blackbirds. Farther up the tree a woodpecker is hard at work. It uses its chisel-like beak to drill a hole in the tree trunk for its home.

Both the wren and the long-tailed tit build ball-shaped nests. There is a tiny entrance hole—so small you would think they could never squeeze through.

Along the branch of the tree are two cup-shaped nests. One is owned by the tiny ruby-throated hummingbird, found only in the Americas. The other belongs to the golden oriole. It has cleverly hung its cup from the fork of a branch.

Weaverbirds, relatives of the house sparrow, live in Africa, Asia, and Australia. One kind weaves a hanging nest with a funnel-shaped entrance at the bottom, so snakes and other enemies cannot get in. The picture shows how the nest is built.

At the bottom of the page are four birds that make their nests on the ground. The bittern builds its home among the marsh reeds. The pheasant and the plover lay their eggs in small hollows in the ground. The sand martin digs a hole in the side of a sandy bank.

bittern

pheasant

7

The Master Builder

Beavers are the cleverest home builders of all animals. The beaver's house is called a lodge, and it is built of logs and mud. Beaver families build their homes in a pond or a lake.

From a distance the lodge looks like a large mound of sticks and earth. The beavers first build a platform of logs and mud until it stands above the water level.

Beavers use the little finger on each hand like a human thumb to get a firm grip on sticks and branches.

6

On top of the platform they build a dome-shaped room. The beavers enter their home by swimming through underwater tunnels. In this way the lodge is safe from enemies such as wolves or bears, who cannot get in.

If the beavers cannot find a lake, they may make one by building a dam across a stream. To make a dam, the beavers cut down small trees by gnawing at the wood with their strong front teeth. Many trees grow near the water and fall into it when the beavers cut them down. The trees are then floated into position. If the trees are some distance away, the beavers have to dig canals to float the trees to the place where they are building their dam.

The beavers fill in the spaces between the logs with a kind of cement made of clay and leaves. If the dam is damaged, all the beavers go to work at once to repair it.

Beavers feed on the bark and young shoots of trees. During the summer they store a lot of food in the water around the lodge. This lasts them through the winter.

Beavers make their homes in the United States and Canada. Some beavers also live in northern Europe. But most European beavers do not build dams and lodges. They live in holes dug in riverbanks.

7

reed warbler

kingfisher

geese

great crested grebe

teal

dragonfly

ramshorn snail

snail egg

8

Graham Allen.

Pond Homes

Many animals make their homes in or near a pond. Hidden among the reeds there may be a great crested grebe's nest made of grass. The reed warbler weaves its nest among the stems, well above the water. Other pond birds include kingfishers, geese, and teals.

Some fish build nests too. The male three-spined stickleback makes a nest for the female to lay her eggs in. First he sucks up mouthfuls of gravel to make a hole at the bottom of the pond. Then he builds an arch of pond weed over the hole to form a tunnel. When the female has laid her eggs, he guards the nest until the eggs hatch.

Some animals spend only part of their lives in a pond. Caddis flies lay their eggs on the water. When the eggs hatch, soft little animals called caddis worms come out. These caddis worms build themselves cases to protect their soft bodies. Each kind of caddis worm builds a particular kind of case. Some use grains of sand cemented together; others use twigs or leaves. Most of these case homes can be moved about, but some caddis worms cement their houses onto large stones. Some weave a silken net to trap food.

The picture shows several other animals that live in ponds. They include snails, newts, frogs, water boatmen, pond skaters, mosquitoes, and diving beetles. Diving beetles use their back legs like oars. The dragonfly hovering over the pond is hunting for food. It catches insects with its front legs. A dragonfly's early life is spent as a nymph, or grub, in the pond.

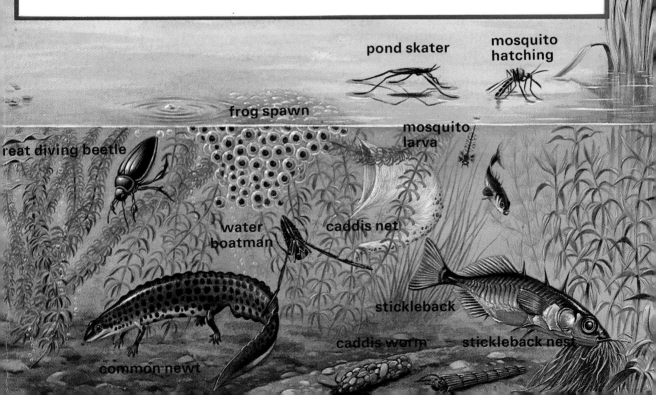

pond skater

mosquito hatching

frog spawn

mosquito larva

great diving beetle

water boatman

caddis net

stickleback

caddis worm

stickleback nest

common newt

Ants and Termites

Most ants build wonderful nests. Some make their nests in the ground or under stones. Others build mounds. Each nest is a maze of tunnels with rooms leading from them. In one nest, thousands of ants live and work together as a group called a colony.

The colony is ruled by the queen, who lives in a room in the middle of the nest. She spends all her time laying eggs. Most of the other ants are workers. They repair the nest, carry the eggs to special rooms to hatch, and look after the young. Other workers hunt for food. When ants meet, they rub their antennae, or feelers, together to find out whether they are strangers or from the same nest.

Many ants keep small insects called aphids, just like farmers keep cows. Aphids make a juice which ants enjoy. The ants milk the aphids by stroking them.

Weaver ants from the tropics build their nests high above the ground by "sewing" leaves together. You can see them in the small picture opposite.

In the other small picture are huge mound nests built by termites. Termites look like ants and are sometimes called white ants, but they are not closely related.

termite nests

Graham Allen

weaver ants

aphids

11

Homes Underground

A great many animals make their homes underground. Few enemies can get in and the homes are warm and cozy.

A badger's home is called a set. Each set has several entrances and many passages and rooms. The tidy badgers keep the set clean by taking all their rubbish outside.

The home of a fox is called an earth. The fox likes to borrow its home rather than to dig it. Sometimes a fox takes over an old badger set. But it does not keep it as clean and tidy as the badger.

Rabbits dig burrows which are a maze of rambling tunnels. A group of burrows is called a warren. A mother rabbit digs a special burrow in which to have her babies. She lines the burrow with hay and with fur from her own body.

The bumblebee builds wax cells for her eggs in a small hole—perhaps an old mouse hole.

Moles spend most of their time underground. They dig tunnels with their strong front feet, pushing the soil away with their back feet. Slugs hide underground during the day so that the sun does not dry them up. Earthworms burrow by swallowing the soil.

fox

rabbit

badger

mole

lug earthworm bumblebee

13

Atkinson

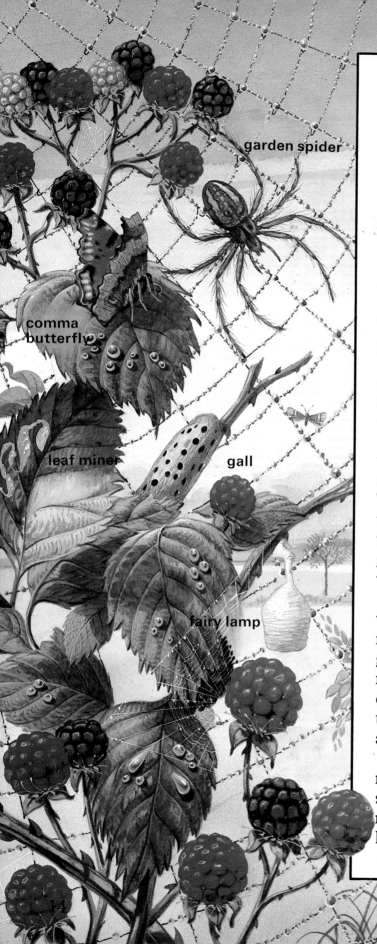

garden spider

comma butterfly

leaf miner

gall

fairy lamp

Garden Homes

You can find all sorts of animals living in the garden, if you know where to look for them.

On an autumn morning, when everything sparkles with dew, look out for the beautiful web spun by the garden spider. It is made from silken thread and shaped like a wheel. The spider uses its web to catch its prey. In autumn, the spider spins a little ball of silk that looks like cotton candy. She lays hundreds of eggs in it. Some spider cocoons are called fairy lamps.

Sometimes you can see little woody lumps or growths on the stems of plants such as brambles. These are called galls. Galls are the homes of young insects when they are larvae, or grubs. The grubs from the gall in the picture will grow into gall wasps.

Near the gall you can see a leaf with wiggly lines on it. These marks are made by a very tiny grub. It burrows inside the thickness of the leaf, just as a coal miner digs tunnels in the ground. Later, the leaf miner becomes a moth and flies away.

Down on the ground live many more animals. You won't often see the hedgehog because it hunts mostly at night. If you turn over a log or a piece of rotten wood, you may see centipedes and millipedes scurrying about as fast as their many legs will carry them. These creatures do not like the light. Nor do the woodlice that share their damp, dark home.

The piece of rotten wood may be covered with tiny holes. These are made by the wood beetle, whose grubs chew long passages in the wood. The beetles bite their way out of the wood and fly away, leaving little holes which show where the grubs lived.

The nests of most garden birds are well hidden, but the house martin's nest is easy to see. It builds a cup-shaped nest of mud just under the eaves of a house. The nest is very strong and is well protected from the wind and rain. So the house martin can use the same nest year after year.

wood beetle and grub

house martin

ane fly

chrysalis

caterpillar

red admiral

hedgehog

garden snail

millipede

centipede

woodlouse

15

Borrowers and Sharers

Animals often share their homes with other animals of their own kind. But some animals live in homes with quite different kinds of creatures. Most of these arrangements are friendly—but some lodgers are a nuisance.

On the left of the picture, a starling family has built a nest on the edge of an eagle's large, untidy home. But the eagle takes no notice of the little birds as it brings back a rabbit for its young to eat. The starling's family has nothing to fear with the eagle nearby.

At the bottom of this page a rattlesnake is lodging in the home of a marmot, a little animal that digs a burrow in the ground. The rattlesnake will use the burrow for its winter sleep, called hibernation. The marmot does not seem to mind its dangerous guest—but it wisely moves over to another part of the burrow.

On the right, a reed warbler has a very unwelcome guest indeed. It is a cuckoo. The cuckoo does not build a nest of her own. She always lays her eggs in another bird's nest. In the bottom of the picture you can see her removing one of the reed warbler's eggs to make room in the nest for her own egg. When the baby cuckoo hatches, it pushes the other eggs out of the nest. The reed warbler feeds the big baby cuckoo as if it were her own chick.

Below is another creature that does not make its own home. Instead, the hermit crab moves into the empty shell of a dead sea snail. On the outside of the shell is a sea anemone. It can catch food from the water as the crab moves around. In return, the sea anemone helps to hide the crab from its enemies.

reed warbler

cuckoo

sea anemone

17

The Beehive

Honeybees, like ants, live and work together in huge colonies. But there are few honeybees in the wild. Instead, most of these useful insects are kept by beekeepers for their honey. The bees live in wooden hives. Each hive has a queen bee, male bees, and workers. The queen bee is much larger than the rest of the bees in the hive and spends most of her time laying eggs. The male bees are called drones. They do not work at all. The worker bees are very busy.

Inside the hive they build a honeycomb of six-sided cells. The cells are made of wax that comes from the bees' bodies. Some of the

grubs

worker bees

eggs

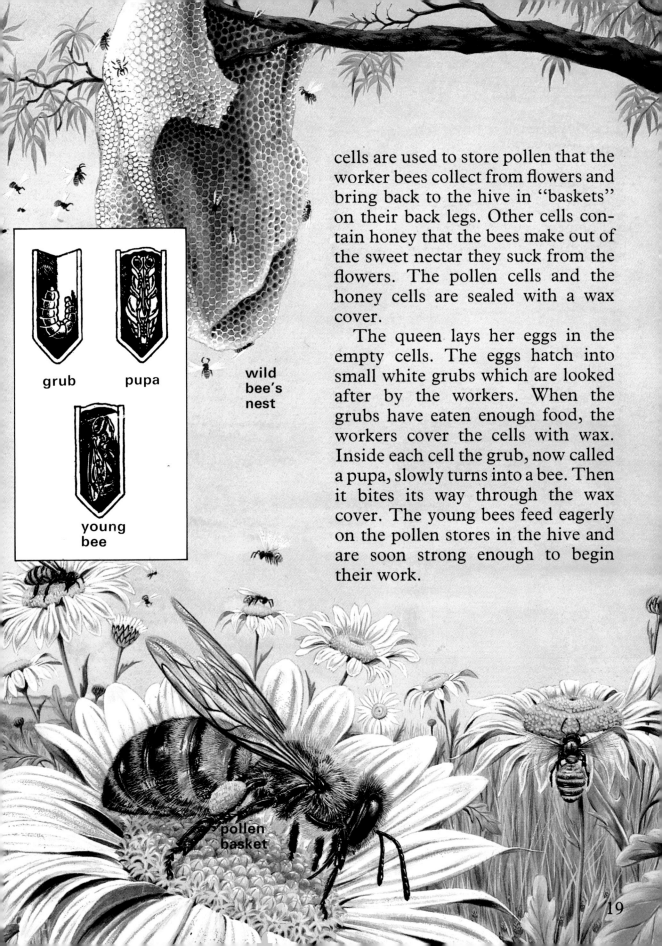

grub

pupa

young
bee

wild
bee's
nest

pollen
basket

cells are used to store pollen that the worker bees collect from flowers and bring back to the hive in "baskets" on their back legs. Other cells contain honey that the bees make out of the sweet nectar they suck from the flowers. The pollen cells and the honey cells are sealed with a wax cover.

The queen lays her eggs in the empty cells. The eggs hatch into small white grubs which are looked after by the workers. When the grubs have eaten enough food, the workers cover the cells with wax. Inside each cell the grub, now called a pupa, slowly turns into a bee. Then it bites its way through the wax cover. The young bees feed eagerly on the pollen stores in the hive and are soon strong enough to begin their work.

On the Seashore

The seashore is a home for many different creatures. When the tide comes in, their home is in salt water. When it goes out, they are left in the open.

Many seashore animals can live out of water when the tide is out. Barnacles, mussels, and limpets are protected by their shells. The barnacle anchors itself to a rock with a kind of cement. The limpet grips the rock with its strong "foot." The mussel holds on to rocks with strong threads from its body.

The scallop has a large and handsome shell. It lives attached to a rock when it is young, then swims away. Whelks crawl along the sand and rocks like snails.

Some seashore animals bury themselves in the sand when the tide is out. The parchment worm makes a U-shaped burrow. The razor shell burrows very quickly, and you will be lucky to see a live one. The tellin burrows into the sand and pushes long tubes called siphons up to the surface to pick up bits of food.

Starfish and sea cucumbers bury themselves deep in the sand or hide in rock pools. Little periwinkles wedge themselves in rock cracks. A

mussels

winkles

bristle worm

sea fan

limpets

sea urchin

capshell

barnacle

scallop

sea anemone

peacock worm

rock-bor piddock

20

small hole in a rock may have been made by the rock-boring piddock shown in the picture. And under rocks near the sea you may find a spiny sea urchin.

When the tide is out, you may see a forest of little tubes. These belong to peacock worms. When the tide is in, each worm unfolds a fan of tentacles to catch food.

The tern nests in a little hollow on the shore, among rocks and sand. The eider duck builds a nest of seaweed, moss, and twigs on the shore. It covers its eggs with its soft, downy feathers. These feathers are often used to make quilts and comforters.

common tern

eider duck

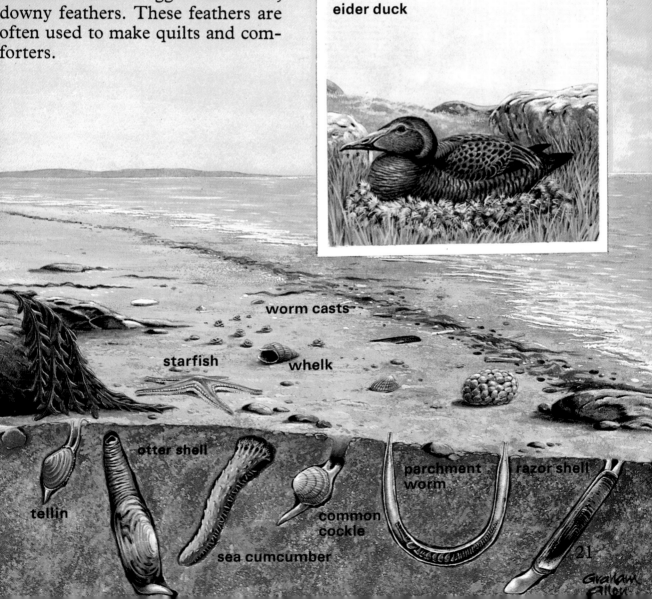

worm casts

starfish

whelk

otter shell

tellin

sea cumcumber

common cockle

parchment worm

razor shell

21

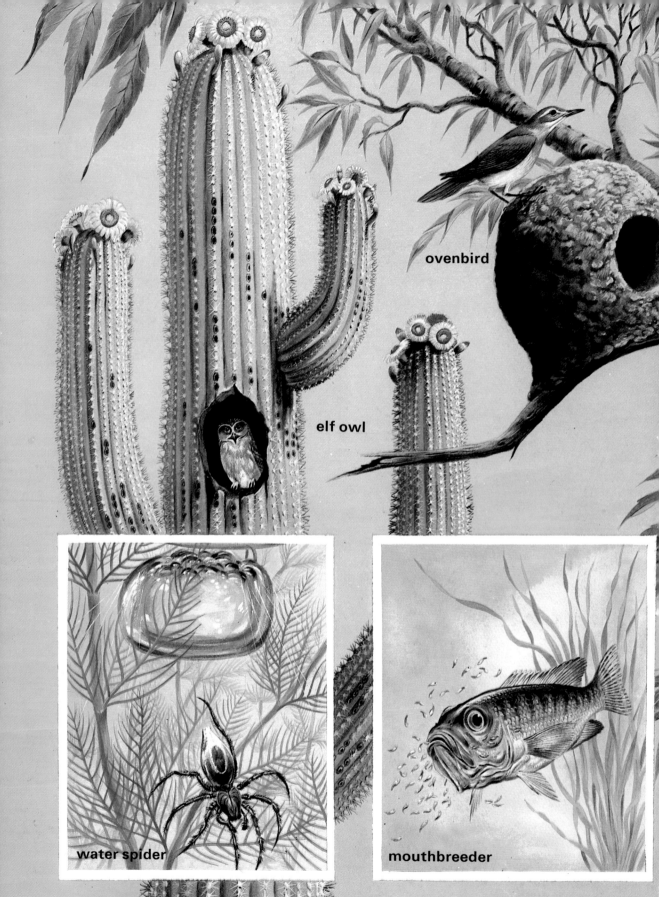

ovenbird

elf owl

water spider

mouthbreeder

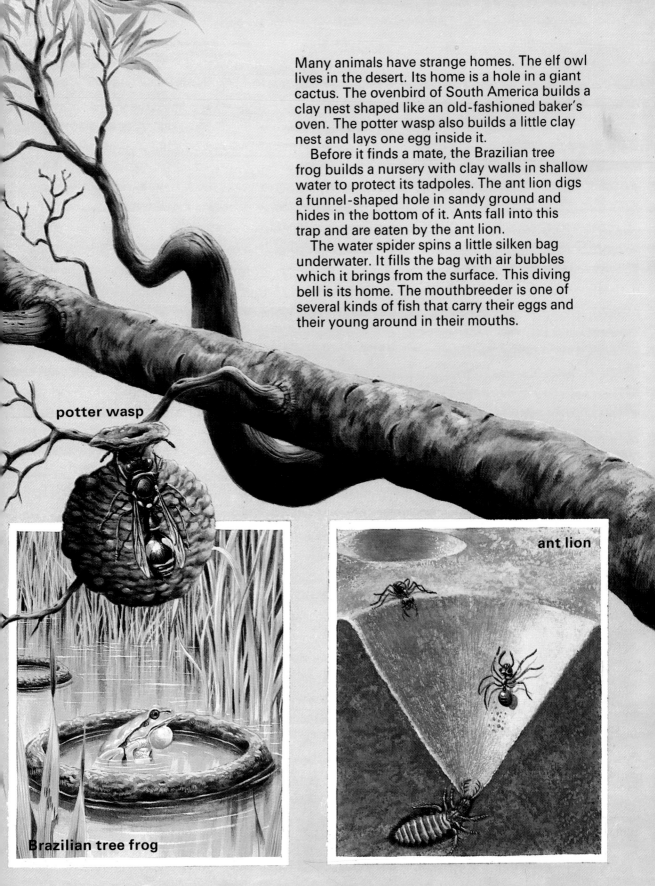

Many animals have strange homes. The elf owl lives in the desert. Its home is a hole in a giant cactus. The ovenbird of South America builds a clay nest shaped like an old-fashioned baker's oven. The potter wasp also builds a little clay nest and lays one egg inside it.

Before it finds a mate, the Brazilian tree frog builds a nursery with clay walls in shallow water to protect its tadpoles. The ant lion digs a funnel-shaped hole in sandy ground and hides in the bottom of it. Ants fall into this trap and are eaten by the ant lion.

The water spider spins a little silken bag underwater. It fills the bag with air bubbles which it brings from the surface. This diving bell is its home. The mouthbreeder is one of several kinds of fish that carry their eggs and their young around in their mouths.

potter wasp

ant lion

Brazilian tree frog

23

Graham Allen.

Index

Numbers in *italics* refer to illustrations.

Revised edition, 1987

Copyright © 1978, 1987 by Grisewood & Dempsey Ltd.

All rights reserved under International and Pan-American Copyright Conventions. Published in the United States by Random House, Inc., New York, and simultaneously in Canada by Random House of Canada Limited, Toronto. This edition first published in Great Britain by Kingfisher Books Limited, a Grisewood & Dempsey Company, in 1987. Originally published in small-format paperback by Pan Books Ltd. in 1978.

Library of Congress Cataloging-in-Publication Data:
Rowland-Entwistle, Theodore.
  Animal homes.
  (Random House all-about books)
  Includes index.
  SUMMARY: Describes a variety of dwellings that animals build, borrow, and share.
  1. Animals—Habitations—Juvenile literature.
[1. Animals—Habitations] l. Allen, Graham, 1940—, ill. II. Title. III. Series.
QL756.R69 1987 591.5'6 86-26145
ISBN: 0-394-88974-6 (trade);
0-394-98974-0 (lib. bdg.)
Manufactured in Spain   1 2 3 4 5 6 7 8 9 0